A PET CAT of your own

James Allcock has over thirty years' experience as a vet and is the principal of a mixed practice in Bristol. He is adviser to Bristol Corporation and has been on the council of the British Veterinary Association for the past twelve years. He appears regularly on radio and television programmes including *Farming Today*, *Woman's Hour*, and *Nationwide*. He also writes a regular column for *Woman's Realm*. James Allcock lives in Avon (or Somerset as he still prefers to call it), and is married with four children. He is the author of *A Pet Dog of Your Own* and *A Pet Bird of Your Own*.

A PET CAT of your own

James Allcock

Illustrated by Mike Morris

SHELDON PRESS
LONDON

First published in Great Britain in 1980 by
Sheldon Press, Marylebone Road, London NW1 4DU

Second impression (Revised edition) 1982
Fourth impression 1988

Copyright © James Allcock, 1980

Printed in Great Britain at
The Camelot Press Ltd, Southampton

ISBN 0 85969 315 5

Contents

Acknowledgements

To veterinary surgeons Mike Findlay, Dixon Gunn, Neal King and Mike Stockman all of whom read, and whose suggestions improved, the text. To Jenny Botsford who typed, punctuated and spelled. To Mike Morris who drew the cartoons which expressed in a very small area the ideas that I took a lot of words to convey, and to Sheldon Press—so efficient and kind with it.

and
Dedicated to all those above—because I've had so many cats that to select one would be most unfair.

Foreword

In writing *A PET CAT of your own*, the second book in the Sheldon Press 'Choosing and Caring for your Pet' series, Jim Allcock has ably demonstrated that his first success with *A PET DOG of your own* can be repeated for cat owners.

The author's knowledge of the nature and behaviour of cats is extensive. He uses this with humour and understanding, the same approach Jim Allcock employs for all his many activities, which involve the public relations side of the British Veterinary Association, the cultivation of orchids and his work in his veterinary practice. For above all Jim Allcock is a vet and he writes with the sure knowledge that the information he passes on is well founded in fact, whether it be the necessary anatomical detail, or the description of a cat's behaviour when ill or distressed.

The information is presented in a most readable style and because the author is by nature a teacher, the observant reader will note that certain important facts are repeated in different chapters. These facts are introduced each time from a different angle and their reappearance seems only to complete the circle of information and emphasize their usefulness.

Readers with a wide experience of cats will enjoy this book as they will find so much with which to agree. Less-experienced owners will recognize many of the truths and be pleased with the concise explanations. Novice cat people will find their questions answered, hopefully before finding out that they are not cat people and adding to our already considerable problem of feral cats. In this context can I particularly recommend the advice on neutering of cats both male and female; advice based on sound physiological and social reasons.

The cartoons of Mike Morris add to the pleasure of this book, highlighting so well how we see our cats, even if they do not see themselves in quite this way.

Knowing of Jim Allcock's family menagerie, and having enjoyed his dog book and his cat book, I can only wonder which he will choose next, the pony, the budgerigar or the Chinese quail.

S. D. Gunn
President, British Veterinary Association

Should you?

If you have reached this far you like cats, which is the best reason for keeping one. But keeping any pet is like having a man about the house. There are some great advantages, you've got company, he's pleasant for most of the time and the mice are frightened of him. On the other side of the coin he makes extra work and at times is untidy and even messy if he's not properly house trained.

If you want a pet about the house, as distinct from in a cage, the only reasonable choices are cats or dogs or both. There are people who keep free-living monkeys, chipmunks, tortoises and even pet hens loose in their homes. It's nearly impossible to house train any of these and such 'offbeat' animal keeping is usually a menace to the humans concerned and rarely, if ever, suitable for the pet.

Liking cats is not enough. In fact, if you like them and respect them, you must consider whether your home and your life style are suitable for a cat. If you spend two or three nights each week away from home, if your normal homecoming is nearer to midnight than 7 p.m. and you leave home just about dawn, then no cat is likely to find you a suitable owner. If you want to keep any living things the choice in these circumstances is probably limited to goldfish or house plants.

There are many situations, however, when owning a dog is not reasonable but you can offer a very acceptable life to a cat. Flat dwellers—out all day—should not contemplate a dog; but in certain circumstances a cat—or better still two cats, as company for each other—might be provided with an acceptable life.

'Certain circumstances' sounds like the words of a

You need time ... certainly to talk to him ...

politician at election time. Let's try to be specific. Sometimes a tenancy agreement excludes dogs but cats are allowed. More important, what is acceptable to the cat? He should have access to the great out-doors, and not just occasionally. A cat-door or cat-flap is essential, which means that proper cat keeping is almost impossible if you live in a single unit on the ninth floor of a purpose-built block of flats. Cats can't work the lift buttons and they're not popular on the stairs.

If your ninth-floor flat is a penthouse with a well-fenced roof garden or balcony then the great out-doors are provided and cats, in the plural, can enjoy life here. Less modern, less pretentious flats offer greater scope for good cat keeping. Ground-floor flats are no problem—except persuading the landlord that a cat-door is needed. First-floor flats and higher will tax your ingenuity but it's often possible to find a route over a sloping roof that allows a cat-window to become accessible to any cat of average ability. Many cats will learn to climb a cat-ladder that is too flimsy to be of the slightest help to any ill-intentioned cat burglar.

Of course there are risks in allowing your cat to come and go at will. The section on accidents expands on this. However, there's an equal, or greater risk of keeping a flat-bound cat in a state of total boredom, punctuated by a very few minutes of feeding each day.

You don't have to take time exercising your cat, but you do need time to feed him, maybe to groom him and certainly to talk to him.

Most first-time cat owners are attracted by a kitten—lively, active, entertaining, dependent. Remember that the kitten becomes a cat. He's a kitten for the first six months that you have him and a cat for the next fourteen years. So if you simply want a kitten for entertainment, don't start. Watch the television cartoons instead.

What sort?

There are nearly sixty varieties of cats and new ones keep appearing, but as a family pet the standard British short-haired cat is best, the good old English 'moggie'. (Scottish or Welsh if you're nationalists.) A short-haired cat means a lot less combing, and it's worth contemplating the advantages of dark-coloured cats because their hairs are less obvious on the furniture, your dinner jacket or little black dress.

The 'exotic' cats, Burmese, Siamese, Persian, make equally good pets but in a different way. The long-haired ones are very demanding of time to keep them smart and the Siamese/Burmese group have a different temperament and attitude to life.

Nearly 95 per cent of all cats in this country are non-pedigree and it is very likely that the first 'cat of your own' will be (should be) one of these. Pedigree cats of the 'exotic' breeds are outside the scope of this book. If you are attracted to them, first find the owner of such a cat and learn, by meeting the cat, the attractions that these breeds offer.

How many?

There is a lot in favour of a pair of cats—pair in the two sense—not necessarily male and female. In any event the majority of house cats become 'its' so sex is relatively unimportant—in this context at least.

Two cats are company for each other, especially if you have to leave them for parts of the day. When they are kittens, each provides a playmate for the other and as older cats they provide reinforcements if another unfriendly neighbourhood cat tries to take over their territory. The playmate theory does not always work well, however. One veterinary surgeon taking part in a radio 'phone-in' was asked for advice about a cat which persistently chewed up pot plants growing in the house. The instant answer of 'You've got a bored cat; he needs company; why not get another kitten so that the two cats can play with each other' appeared very acceptable to the listener. About six months later the same caller phoned the same vet, who was doing the same 'phone-in' to say, 'You advised me, when my cat was eating the plants, that he was bored and suggested a kitten as company. I got one, now there are two cats eating the house plants!' No instant answer this time.

Now there are two cats eating the pot plants!

What sex?

Although you will almost certainly have your cat neutered, you should consider which one you are going to choose. Gentlemen first. Castration of tom cats is less expensive than spaying the female. The male usually grows rather bigger. If any bladder trouble develops, the male anatomy makes this a potentially more serious condition than the same trouble in the female.

With apologies for the delay—Ladies. She cats may be marginally gentler, neutering (spaying) is more costly, and of course they can have a litter before spaying. One of the benefits of pet keeping in a family is the instruction and experience that pets give to children in matters of sex, birth, death and consideration for all things living. If you keep an unspayed female cat she will almost inevitably have kittens and this experience is one of the good reasons for keeping pets and children together. Spaying after one litter is quite normal so you're not committed to a continuous supply of new-born kittens.

How much?

All pleasures have to be paid for, and there is a bill for the pleasure of owning a cat. Cat owning is not an expensive pleasure but be certain that you want to pay the costs of cat owning before you indulge yourself.

Kittens are often free of charge. More kittens are born than homes are available and from May to September there is usually a surplus of kittens 'free to good homes', as the showcase postcards put it. From November to March there are many less kittens and you may not find free ones. £2–10 is the sort of price that you will pay for the British short-haired kitten. The pedigree cat may cost anything from £40 to £120 for one of 'pet' standard. Potential show specimens of the rare or popular breeds may cost £200 or more, but these are for the show enthusiast or breeder.

Having got—be it by gift or purchase—your kitten, there are some other expenses apart from food.

Inoculations are essential. The minimum inoculation against feline enteritis costs about £9 to £10 and the flu and enteritis injections about £16–£22.

Neutering is usual during the first year and is definitely non-recurring. It costs about £10–£15 for the male and £18–£24 for the female.

A comb and food and water bowls are essential. We're only talking about £5 or so in total and you may well have suitable food dishes already, but do keep the cat's food dishes for the cat.

Cat box or bed. Your cat will have to sleep somewhere so you might buy a bed for him. On the other hand, the young kitten—and the older cat—are very happy in a cardboard box with newspaper as bedding. It's warm, the cat feels secure and you can change the bedding every day, with yesterday's paper, and the box every week after you have taken the groceries out of it. A box or basket for travel is a different matter. It's very useful, and almost essential to have one. Cats loose in motor cars are not conducive to safety on the roads and you will have to take your cat to your vet or to boarding kennels on a number of occasions through his life. This cat box can be a simple cardboard 'Pet Pack'; many vets and pet shops have them. The cost is not much more than £2 so if it gets dirty or messy, throw it away and buy a new one. Wicker baskets cost £15 or more, and plastic-covered wire ones, which cats seem to prefer, or even the more up-market polished wood and perspex carriers, are £25 upwards. One of these alternatives is much better than an old cardboard box tied with string.

Boarding for the cat may be another cost when you go on holiday. Allow at least £2·50 per day for each day in kennels.

Veterinary fees have to be paid sometimes. Cats are healthy animals and after the initial inoculations and neutering, many cats need little veterinary attention apart from annual or biennial booster inoculations. But accidents do happen, infections appear and in time every cat suffers from the troubles of old age. £20 per year will cover all this for the average cat and, apart from boosters, quite a few cats never see a vet for years on end. But you might have an unlucky cat, or you might even be a hypochondriac owner, so be prepared for some cost, and the £20 per year average might mean that £80 or more is the bill for one major illness or accident repair.

Feeding is the biggest and continuing expense. You can make feeding expensive if you insist on buying fillet steak or rabbit, but there's no need to. In fact, this sort of food alone is not a very good diet. If you feed one of the standard proprietary cat foods, the cost is about 30p per day.

So on the traditional 'one sheet of paper' we get:

Capital cost	High	Low
Kitten	£120	Nil
Comb, bed, carrying box, feed dishes	£50	£7
Running costs		
Inoculations (1st year)	£22 (flu and enteritis)	£16 (enteritis only)
Neutering	£24 (female)	£10 (male)
Boarding	£75 (1 month)	Nil
Feeding	£150	£70
Veterinary fees	£100 (bad luck)	Nil (lucky cat)
	£541	£103

Thus the capital cost of starting with a cat can vary between £7 and £170 and the first year costs might be more than £10 per week or below £2. The least expensive cat can well be the pleasantest companion and just as contented and well kept as the top-cost one.

Where from?

Decision made—you want a cat. Not only would you like to keep one but you're prepared for the cost and prepared to take the trouble and time needed to look after a contented, well-kept cat. Where do you find the kitten?

The very best place from which to get the kitten is his mother's home. This way the kitten leaves mother and comes directly to you. This change is a stressful one for any young thing, but a single change of home is so much better and easier for the kitten than the double change involved if you get one from a cats' home or a pet shop. When you get a young kitten he should be about seven or eight weeks old and to ask him to cope with two changes of home in this very short period of life is too much.

If you can find a kitten that's been born into a household of children, you'll get a gentle kitten, and if you get a kitten born wild and never handled until he's eight weeks old, he'll always be a difficult cat. Early handling appears to accustom a cat to the human and if a kitten has been stroked, petted and picked up by children from the age of two or three weeks, he will accept this for ever. Now someone, with the best of motives, is going to be horrified at the thought of children 'molesting' young kittens. Have faith in the kitten—and this also applies if you bring a young kitten into the family. Of course very rough handling of a kitten can cause injury, and accidents occur when a kitten falls from someone's arms, but such happenings are rare. The 'over-loved' kitten protects himself by scratching quite effectively and it is amazing how kittens appear to enjoy being handled, and not only by humans. Once a whippet bitch was seen carrying six-week-old kittens about by

their heads. There was panic on the part of the owner
and the chastened whippet was sent away. Of course
she was back within a very few minutes, but not
before the kittens had set off in search of her to continue this game. Don't judge by superficial appear-
ances; judge by reactions; so very often you'll find
kittens like attention in the oddest guise.

So far we've decided to find a kitten from his
mother's home. But how do you find mother? In the
spring and early summer it's easy. There are always
more kittens than homes at this time of year. You
may hear on the grapevine that Mrs Bloggins' cat's
had kittens; your children may bring this type of information home from school. Postcard adverts in
shop windows are always interesting—and sometimes offer kittens. Many veterinary surgeons keep a
list of 'kittens for homes'.

By one means or another you discover a kitten
source. Then you go and see the kitten. At this stage
leave all sentimentality behind. You are trying to find
a fit, healthy kitten, old enough to leave his mother
and of the appropriate sex. Do not, if you can so
steel yourself, take a scrawny, scruffy, flea-ridden,
dirty-tailed kitten because you are sorry for him.
This is a hard-hearted counsel of perfection, but if
you take on this unhealthy waif, you will certainly
spend a considerable amount of time and some
amount of money in turning him into a healthy
cat. Worst of all, you might fail and either lose the
kitten or find that you have acquired a chronic
invalid.

Let's list the common faults of young kittens and
try and make an 'importance' list.

General bodily condition.   A kitten should feel
plump and heavy. In actual weight he should be at
least 1½lb at six weeks old. This is the youngest age

any kitten should leave mother. Eastern cats such as Siamese and Burmese will weigh less. Reject a skinny, near-emaciated kitten.

Eyes, nose. There should be no sneezing, runny nose or runny eyes. Both eyes should be wide open and clean. Reject any kitten with bad eyes.

Tail end. Look for signs of diarrhoea—wet tail or a sore anus. Look for diarrhoea on the floor if the kittens are in a pen or box. Reject kittens with diarrhoea.

Coat should be free from fleas; these are dealt with in more detail later. If there are a few fleas deal with them quickly. Even call in to see your vet on the way home to get safe treatments for a young kitten.

Ears are often infected with ear mites caught from mum. Look in the ear. Dry, dark-brown, mahogany-coloured wax is a sign of mites. Again more in a later chapter, but you can take a kitten with mites in ears, secure in the knowledge that these invaders can be cleared up easily. This may be another situation where a visit to the vet on the way home is worth while.

Extra toes. Some kittens are born with extra toes. There should be four on each foot and a dewclaw (our thumb) on the inside of each front leg. The extra-toed kitten might have any number of extras, up to ten toes per foot. One or two extra are a nuisance (the nails often grow too long) but many kittens develop into good cats and live to a ripe old age with one toe too many. It's difficult to make a hard and fast rule about this. One rule you should know is that cats with extra toes are not accepted at any cat shows.

Colour. We all know that black cats are lucky. That's a matter of faith. There are some matters of fact connected with colour.

Tortoiseshell cats, with black, white and ginger in the coat, are always female.

Ginger cats are most often male but this is not an invariable situation. You can sex a tortoiseshell cat from a very long distance away. You can bet at evens that a ginger is male, and with enough bets you'll make money, but you won't win them all.

White cats are sometimes deaf, and often have eyes of different colours, one eye green, one eye yellow— no detriment to the cat.

This sounds as if every kitten is an unhealthy, flea-ridden disaster. That's not so at all, but there are some gift kittens that no one has looked at very closely, and the gift turns out to be a heartbreak. It's not only gift horses you should look in the mouth—and elsewhere.

If you're buying a pedigree kitten from an experienced breeder there should be no problems, but even here be choosy. Don't accept anything that's less than perfect. Don't believe 'that's only a cold, it will soon clear' or 'all kittens scratch their ears and have fleas'. If you like the scratching, sneezing kitten, accept it only later on when the breeder/seller has cleared up the sneezing and got rid of the fleas or source of scratching. Don't forget your vet in all this. Take the kitten to him before you buy it. He'll advise you about the 'best buy'. Cost of such an examination at his surgery will be about £5–£6, very little if you're buying a pedigree cat and very good value for peace of mind if you're taking on a 'free' kitten.

Sexing

Even though your kitten will spend most of its life as a neutered 'it', you probably want to know the sex. It is surprising how much confusion occurs in this very basic determination. Every practising veterinary surgeon knows, and accepts, that some of the tom cats booked in for castration will turn out to be female on arrival at the surgery, and the reverse error is even more common. Sexing is not difficult but you must look at the right end. It's not enough to decide that your kitten has a feminine face, any more than one can decide about the young, long-haired, bejeaned human at anything but close range.

Look at the rear view (we're back to kittens now). Put the kitten on a table and raise the tail. You'll see one of two views:

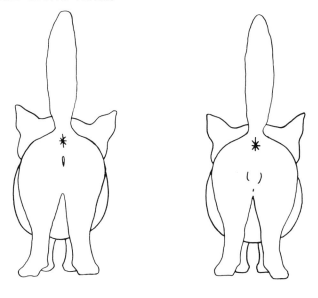

QUEEN   TOM

Vive la différence!

Cats and dogs

Quite a number of the much-loved family cats did not start—in that family at least—as kittens. Cats, much more than dogs, tend to appear and adopt you. Adult cats need homes because their owners are moving, leaving the country, or even have died. Let's just consider starting with an adult cat. If the cat finds you—that is, appears on the doorstep—decide very quickly if this is to be the start of a beautiful friendship. Don't be unfair to the cat by starting to feed him, and after one or two weeks, try to chase him away because you don't want a cat (or that cat) anyhow.

Try to be somewhat selective about the 'walk-in' cat if you are thinking in pet terms. A lone feral cat, born and brought up away from humans, will rarely if ever domesticate. He may learn to take food that you supply, he may come into the house, but it's most unlikely that you will be able to stroke him or pick him up without some bloodletting on your part. Befriend this cat by all means, let him know that you keep a good table, but you are entertaining a visitor rather than adopting a pet.

On the other hand, the cat that comes to see you, walks in as if he owns the house, curls up by the fire and expects to be stroked is potentially a first-class pet. It could be that he has a home nearby and has simply come out for a walk, but it is surprising how many of these friendly visitors never return whence they came or are not claimed by their owner.

Be selective again about the 'gift' cat—the one to which you set out to give food and shelter. Is he apparently healthy, flea-free, neutered, inoculated (and ask when and if there is a certificate)? Don't—unless you want to—take on a chronic invalid.

Two things cause heart searching and worry if you get a new cat, or if you are moving house and taking your cat with you—as you should do.

First. How do I get him established so that he won't stray? This does not in fact seem to be a great problem, but in the owner's imagination it is an unscalable mountain. The oft-repeated advice to butter the paws is of very doubtful value. Cats don't like oily paws and the pitter of butter-patted feet on your carpets will benefit neither the Wilton nor the Axminster. If you keep him indoors for the first twenty-four hours (provide a dirt tray) and then just before feeding time, when the cat is worrying you asking for food, let him out for the first time, the prospect of food will bring him back quickly. Continue this strategy (or should it be these tactics—I never studied military terms) for the first ten days or so, gradually extending the interval before food.

Secondly. How do I introduce him to my other cat/dog already in possession of the house? The answer is slowly, quietly, and, most important, DON'T INTERFERE. Any group of animals has a social order. One is 'boss' and another at the bottom of the ladder. The animals sort it out—how, why, we know not, but human ideas play no part in this. Every vet has seen the large, fierce, bull mastiff treating a tiny kitten with the greatest of respect and deferring to her every wish. The old, rather decrepit she cat will often dominate any younger cats in 'her' house.

Inevitably there will be spats, spits and sparring. Allow space, so that the 'under cat' can retreat with an appearance of dignity. Don't provoke crises by allowing the first, or early, meetings of new and old animals in confined spaces, or when food is at hand. Feed at the same time, but with food dishes well separated, at opposite ends of the room, and with a chair or table between them. If the first introduction

. . . deferring to her every wish

is in a living room, make certain that breakable valuables are safe. Every frightened animal climbs on to a chair, table, sideboard, corner shelf, or what have you.

Acceptance—or is the modern word 'integration'?—of the immigrant will take a few weeks but the worst of the difficulties should be over within the first week and usually the cats or dog and cat(s) will be sharing the hearth—if not their box—within six weeks.

Feeding

Feeding is the fundamental part of cat owning. Whatever else you do you've got to feed him each and every day. Let's dismiss one fallacy to begin with. The hungry cat, the half-fed cat is not a better mouser. He's much more likely to go searching for and scrounging food elsewhere and ignore any mice you may have. The mouse-catching cat hunts for enjoyment, and if he is well fed he will mouse much better.

Cats require more protein than dogs, some animal fats, and have to obtain some of their vitamins ready made; the same vitamins are 'home-made' by the dog. Prepared canned foods form one of the easiest—and cheapest—ways of feeding your cat. *Read the instructions*—because these foods vary in moisture content and concentration. Flavour is a matter of taste—the cat's, not yours—and the fact that the food may smell terrible to you does not matter to the cat; it might seem like manna from heaven to him.

If you do not wish to feed canned food, or use them only part of the time, the diet must be mainly meat or fish, about 6–8 ounces per day, and vary the type of meat. Dietary deficiencies can occur with an all-offal diet, an all-fish diet or an all-rabbit diet. So give red meat one day, fish another, then a couple of ounces of liver with some heart; what's missing in one type of food will be there in the other. Whether the food is cooked or not is not vital; it is useful to alternate, then the cat is not disturbed when raw food is on the menu.

As well as food, your cat needs fluid. Milk is a traditional drink for cats and most like it, sometimes to excess; why else 'the cat that got at the cream'? Unfortunately—like so many things in life—likes are not always the best indication of suitability. Some cats cannot tolerate large quantities of milk—and some cannot tolerate it at all. Diarrhoea is the usual ill-effect—and the resultant lack of control makes house-training difficult and the cat is (unfairly) branded a dirty cat. Beware of milk and if there is any tendency to diarrhoea a 'No milk today', or any day—régime might be the answer to this problem. It's well worth trying if the cat is quite fit in every other respect. But, if diarrhoea occurs and the cat is unwell, off food or shows other symptoms, a proper diagnosis must be made and treatment started—so off to the vet in these circumstances. Even if you provide milk—and certainly if you do not—drinking water is essential. Provide it—leave it to the cat to drink it. Many cats appear to drink very little, but they take a lot of fluid in their food. Canned foods contain quite a proportion of water and so do meat and fish.

Dry cat food is available—and so are a number of fears, fallacies and fabrications about it. For a fourth F, let's try facts.

Because many cats do not drink much and rely on food as a major source of their fluid, there is a possibility that dry food will not provide enough fluid and the cat will not drink enough to make up this water shortage. Because he's not taking enough water, the urine becomes very concentrated and salts in the urine can crystallize out while the urine is in the bladder. These crystals form a sandy material which irritates the lining of the bladder leading to cystitis which is painful and quite serious, in the female cat. In the male it may be even more serious and create a real emergency situation in that the crystalline, sandy material blocks the urethra (the tube from the bladder via the penis to the great outdoors) and the cat cannot pass urine. This is painful, serious and urgent.

In the early days of dry cat foods, there was an excess of magnesium salts in some makes and this crystallizing problem and thus cystitis was more likely. This has been rectified for many years now but the troubles are remembered.

Every packet of dry cat food contains a maker's recommendation to 'Provide clean drinking water at all times'—or words to that effect. Sometimes one might wish the instructions were in larger print but more often one wishes that the cat could read—because some owners don't. But even the educated cat, reading the instructions, need not follow them and there may be an increased risk of over-concentrated urine and so cystitis in some cats fed on a fair quantity of dry cat food. This risk applies only to some cats. So what do you do?

If your cat has ever suffered from any form of bladder trouble, cystitis, or retention of urine it is wise not to feed dry food—and your vet may well have said this to you.

If you are feeding a cat on dry food, and he is enjoying it, and you give him plenty of water, don't change.

If you are starting with a new cat, or a new kitten, and you find the dry foods convenient, cheap and less bumpy to carry home from the supermarket, then feed dry—but not every day—and make sure water is always available.

There is one advantage of dry foods. Cats like to 'crunch' them and this helps to keep the teeth clean.

Inoculations

There are two major diseases that we can inoculate cats against.

Feline enteritis is caused by a virus. Incidentally, we are talking about feline enteritis as a disease. The word 'enteritis' itself simply means an inflammation of the intestine, so if your cat has diarrhoea he could be suffering from an enteritis; but this is not the same thing as the virus disease known as feline enteritis which (back to the point at last) is an acute disease. The cat is very depressed, maybe vomits, sits miserably hunched up and can die within twelve hours in the acute case. Some of the stories of all the cats in a district being poisoned arise from outbreaks of feline enteritis. Treatment is by no means always effective and must be started early to be of any benefit. Prevention is essential. Inoculation usually is done at twelve weeks although it is possible to start sooner. There are rarely, if ever, any ill-effects—or any visible effects—on the kitten after injection.

Cat flu is used for the diseases caused by two separate viruses. The symptoms can vary from a sneezy cold to an acute illness not unlike feline enteritis, although not such a dangerous disease. With early treatment a large percentage of cats recover from flu; nevertheless they have an unhappy few days—so do you—and some are left with catarrh or blocked tear ducts which can be a permanent nuisance. There are two methods of vaccination against flu. One involves injection, the other is by intra-nasal vaccination—that is dropping the vaccine into the cat's nostrils. The usual age for this vaccination is about twelve weeks.

Any new kitten needs to settle in his new home

before either vaccination is given. There is a very good reason for this. If we are aiming to provide any long-lasting immunity—and so protection—for your cat, the injection must be one that stimulates the cat to manufacture his own antibodies. There has to be a positive action on the part of the defence mechanism of the cat. Now, if a new kitten has just changed homes, just changed diets, or is undergoing some stress, he is not capable of producing as effective immunity as the same kitten, two weeks later, who is by then adjusted to the new house, new diet, new everything.

The 'settling in' time is about ten days to a fortnight. By that time your new kitten is no longer 'new' in 'your' house—he's your kitten in his house and ready for anything.

One other thing accompanies inoculation—a certificate. Keep this safely, where you can find it, for two reasons. Almost every boarding cattery will require that your kitten has been vaccinated before accepting him as a boarder. Your word that 'my cat has been vaccinated' is not enough. They want the certificate although—and this is a weakness of many certificates—it merely says that 'a ginger cat, male, 4 months old, named "Marmalade", was vaccinated on 1 June 1979'. Your word that this certificate belongs to this cat is happily accepted. Of course the kennels have the opportunity of checking that the vaccine is recent enough to be still effective and any owner who would bother to 'fiddle' certificates has an odd approach to his responsibilities anyhow.

The second reason for keeping the certificate and reading it is *Booster*. Immunity from vaccination wears out and needs boosting now and again. We see the wear out of immunity in human disease such as an epidemic of influenza. One year there is a lot of flu and every other person you speak to has it, or has had it. Then a few years pass during which there is very little until a new epidemic occurs. The human population had an immunity after the first epidemic and it takes three or four years for immunity to wear out before enough people are susceptible to allow another epidemic to start. Cats can get boosters from natural infection, from the wandering cat, and so enhance their immunity free of charge, but you never know if this has happened. So booster vaccinations are necessary. The timing of boosters varies depending on the particular vaccine used and the particular disease situation in your area. Ask your vet and read the reminder which is usually on the vaccination certificate. As a rough guide—every two years for feline enteritis and possibly every year for the flu vaccine.

Neutering

We are talking about pet cats and neutering is the norm. You may ask why. You may think 'poor cats'. There are a lot of very good reasons, however, for neutering a pet cat. This operation is castration in the male and ovarohysterectomy (spaying) in the female. The she cat, not neutered, produces kittens—a self-evident statement—but she produces them in large numbers and inconveniently frequently. Three litters each of four or five per year are not uncommon, and no matter how large your circle of friends, it's never large enough to provide homes for all these kittens. There is an annual surplus of kittens and many unwanted ones are destroyed each year, so population control alone is a good enough reason for neutering a pet she cat.

There are other reasons also. Constant kitten production is a serious strain on a queen. She is always smaller, often less active, more concerned with kittens than being a pet and her expectation of life is less. While the neutered cat will very often live to fourteen or fifteen years, and many much longer, the reproductive queen rarely passes twelve years.

Heat, more often described as 'calling', is a noisy performance. The cat howls, rolls, squats head down, tail up and sometimes behaves in such a manner as to suggest agony. Every vet in practice has been called out, in a hurry, to the cat in agony which finally turns out to be a she cat on heat. Neutering prevents 'calling' and the domestic disturbance associated with it. Any bright ideas you may have about keeping a cat in to avoid kittens are most often doomed to failure. If mating does not take place, heat recurs every two or three weeks for about eight months of the year and most she cats are cunning and determined enough to get out and get mated at some time. If you do succeed in keeping a cat in the house and chaste for a year, perhaps you could use this as a good reference if you ever apply for a job as adviser on security to a maximum-security prison.

'Calling', one assumes, refers to the cries and calls made by a queen on heat, but there's another sort of calling that constitutes a good reason for neutering: the tom cats that call to pay court to your she cat. These toms have three anti-social habits. They 'yowl', they fight with each other (noisily) and they 'spray' (very pungent urine) about the place, and a lot of this

They 'yowl' ...

activity takes place in the wee small hours—and that's
not a pun on the spraying habits.

Full tom cats, that is, un-neutered males, are very
rarely satisfactory pets. They may stay home for two
or three months before Christmas but for the rest of
the year they're wanderers, worse than any lovelorn
teenager who uses his house as an hotel. The tom cat

... and they 'spray'

takes off for weeks on end returning only when he
needs a rest or has been badly beaten up by other toms
competing for the same lady. When he returns home
he smells—strongly. Because of the journeys that tom
cats undertake, their chances of being hit by motor
cars are considerable. Because they fight with each
other, abscesses are a frequent occurrence and all this
stress, strain and activity means a shorter life span than
for the neutered tom cat.

If these reasons have convinced you that you should have your kitten neutered, the next questions are:

When? Ask your vet; opinions as to the best age vary a little but most seem to agree that about five to six months for the she cat and a little older for the tom cat are suitable minimum ages. The operation can be done at any age after this and, in theory at least, there is no maximum age.

What's involved? In the she kitten the operation is removal of both ovaries and the uterus. A general anaesthetic is used, of course, and the kitten has to stay at the surgery for the day or a day and night. After-effects are negligible and, apart from a slightly dopey kitten on the night after the operation, and some fur clipped off the side, there should be no visible effects at all. The operation is usually done on the flank of the cat although some people prefer the operation in the Siamese to be done in the mid-line underneath the abdomen so that the clipped fur doesn't show if it regrows a different shade, as it sometimes does.

In the male the operation is removal of the testicles. While it is possible to operate using local anaesthetic, a general is more usual and so a day or day and night at the surgery is normal. After-effects are nil and in both sexes recovery seems to be even quicker if the kitten is allowed normal activity the day after the operation.

There is no advantage in doing limited operations such as tying the fallopian tubes in the female or vasectomy in the male. While either operation would be effective as a method of (kitten) birth control, all the anti-social habits, noises, smells and behaviour of the entire animal would remain.

It is possible to prevent heat in she cats by the use of hormone tablets or injections, and if you wish to breed from your queen at some time in the future but not just now, these drugs can save a deal of disturbance and unwanted kittens. Such treatments are not a substitute for spaying once you have made the basic decision not to breed from your cat.

Worms

Worms in cats usually worry the cat owner more than the cat. This doesn't mean that you should ignore worms but it does mean that you must not blame worms for each and every illness of your cat. There may be worms present—you might have seen them—and the cat might be very ill, but the worms may be playing no part in causing this illness.

There are two main types of worms that might get into your cat—and you might see.

Round worms—species of Toxocara. These are called 'round' because they are round in cross-section. You might see the whole worm in faeces or in vomit. It is 2–6 inches long, white to fawn in colour, wiry looking, round in cross-section and often coiled or in a loop shape. The cat catches these worms in the first instance from another cat, maybe from his mother. The worm's life-cycle allows kittens to be infected even before birth. This may sound odd, but here's how it happens. Round worms lay eggs in considerable numbers. These eggs are passed out in the faeces and the egg then develops for about thirty days in soil or similar moist material. At this stage there is a larval worm in the egg shell. If this is eaten by a cat the larva hatches and burrows through the intestine wall; it gets into the bloodstream, travels through the liver, then into the lungs and up the windpipe where the still-developing worm is reswallowed and goes back to the intestine to grow up into an adult worm.

Very rarely a human child will swallow one of these worm larvae. If this happens, the larva usually dies because it has arrived in a strange and unsuitable host; but now and again (maybe ten times a year in the whole of the United Kingdom) the larva will migrate and reach the eye, causing damage to the retina. This is very, very rare and quite possibly a similar worm from the dog causes any cases that occur, and cat worms are not guilty. Good hygiene at all times and regular routine worming of cats and dogs would prevent even these few cases.

It is difficult to put this type of risk in perspective. To the family of the child, and the child to whom it happens, it is a tragedy and vitally important. But more people are struck by lightning each year than suffer a damaged eye from Toxocara; ten people are killed on the roads each day and, believe it or not but it is true, 2,700 people died from choking on steak in the U.S.A. in 1975. End of attempt to quantify a real but minuscule risk.

Tape worms are the other major group of worms, nearly harmless to the cat, but no one likes to see worms. The commonest is called Dipylidium. It is an interesting worm and is usually seen as little segments on the faeces or around the anus and on the hair at the rear end of the cat. These segments are from the mature tail end of the worm. They are full of eggs. The segment dries up and bursts, releasing the eggs. A flea or a louse then eats the egg and a cyst stage develops while the egg is in the flea. The cat eats the flea and a new worm develops.

Fleas, or more rarely lice, are an essential part of the life history of this worm. No fleas—no worms. If a cat, dog, human, giraffe or guinea pig swallowed the worm egg, nothing would happen.

One other distinct character of Dipylidium is that the fresh segments wriggle, and they are the only tape-worm segments with this ability. They are $\frac{1}{4}$–$\frac{1}{2}$ inch long, flattened, and creamy white in colour. In the middle of the wriggle they often appear oval in shape and many owners then think these are round worms, buy a round-worm dose for their cat and complain when the worms continue to appear. Wrong medicine—no results.

Another tape worm, a species of Taenia, can appear. This one has an intermediate host, but instead of fleas or lice lives in small mammals such as voles and shrews. The worm eggs from the cat get into soil and on vegetation which is then eaten by a shrew or vole and a cyst develops. The cat catches and eats his victim and so a new worm can start in your cat. If we could only persuade cats to cook the food they catch, this worm could be eliminated. Until then it's a case of worming the cat regularly, maybe every six to ten weeks.

So far we've talked about worms and their hosts. What do you, the cat owner, do if you think your cat has worms or if you see a worm leave either end of the cat? Don't panic. If an adult round worm is vomited or if tape-worm segments are seen in the dirt box, you can be certain that the now visible worms have been present for many weeks at least, inside the cat, but they have been invisible. The cat hasn't suffered in those weeks so the very fact that you have seen the worm does not make your cat dangerously ill. No one likes worms so it is reasonable to try to remove them. Find out what sort of worm you're dealing with. The descriptions on the previous pages should help you, but if you're not sure, take *the worm* to the vet. Take the cat as well, but there will be a better identification of the worm, and so correct treatment and advice, if the vet can see the worm rather than just the cat and you. A garbled description such as 'It looked like a piece of string—not very long' or 'I didn't like to touch it, so I picked it up on a shovel without looking', are comments that every vet has heard.

Put the worm in a polythene bag so that it doesn't shrivel up. This morning's tape-worm segment can dry up and blow away in a puff of wind if you put it in a matchbox or wrap it in tissue paper.

If you're worried about worms but don't see any, take a sample of faeces to your vet and he will be able to examine this under the microscope, looking for worm eggs. If he doesn't find any, this is not proof positive that your cat is free from worms, but it does mean that there aren't large quantities present. If a second and third sample are also free from worm eggs, then you can presume that the cat is free from worms.

Treatment is usually by tablets but possibly by powder or liquid medicines. You may get them from your vet or from a pet shop or pharmacy. If you buy any worm dose 'over the counter' make sure you get the correct sort; *read* the instructions and follow them.

One other worm, nothing to do with cats or dogs, but one that is found in children, is called Enterobius, the pin worm. This worm is passed from one child to another directly. Dogs and cats cannot carry this worm but sometimes they are blamed by anxious parents, well-meaning grannies and even by medically qualified people. Such blame is unfair to the cat and may well mean that the proper treatment of the child is not instituted.

If you are ever in the situation when your doctor suggests that the cat (or any other pet) might be the source of illness in any of your family, it's worth asking him to tell your vet about the animal involved so that the pet can be examined and investigated and the source for the human trouble proved—or disproved—as the case may be. Often the animal blamed is not the source of infection.

Fleas

Fleas are not at all uncommon on cats, but there is no reason why any well-cared-for cat should have fleas. They are uncomfy for the cat sometimes causing acute allergies, transmit tape worms from cat to cat and occasionally bite humans, not seriously, but embarrassingly.

Fleas

Fleas are dark mahogany in colour, about one-tenth of an inch in size and move quite quickly on the skin. If you catch one, it will jump away. The best place to look for fleas on your cat is at the base of the spine, forward from the tail. If there are no fleas to be found, you might find tiny black specks, rather like coal dust. These are flea faeces and consist of partially digested blood. If you find these black granules when combing and are not sure if they are dust or flea droppings, tip them onto a moist tissue. Within a few minutes a pink/brown stain may appear around each particle as the colouring matter of the blood is dissolved. If this happens, there's no doubt. It is fleas, not the cat visiting the coal cellar.

In order to control fleas, it's necessary to know about their life-cycle. Starting from the adult flea on the cat, this flea mates, then leaves the cat to find some dusty, warm, slightly moist area to lay its eggs. The cat's box, underneath fitted carpets by a radiator, the heap of old socks in the cellar or boiler room are ideal flea maternity homes. The eggs hatch into larvae which develop into young fleas. This takes about thirty days but the process is slowed down in cold conditions. The young fleas can live for many months feeding on dust and debris. Before the young flea becomes mature, he or she must find an animal and thus a feed of blood, and it is only the adult flea that worries your cat.

Any attempt to control fleas must include treatment of the cat's environment as well as the cat.

Fleas are easy to kill, the biggest problem is making contact with them. Dusting powder is most often used to treat the cat. Dust it well in, against the hair, and have the cat under proper control before you start; on a table covered with newspaper is the best way. Don't forget that the cat has an underneath as well as a back and get some powder all over the cat. Comb out the surplus powder on to the newspaper and combings, surplus dusting powder and some dead fleas can be conveniently rolled up in the paper and burnt.

Flea collars, impregnated with insecticides, are useful. A very few cats seem to be allergic to them, so if your cat develops a sore neck after wearing a flea collar, it's not for him. There's one other situation where it's wise to avoid flea collars also—if there are any toddling children about. Junior grabs the flea collar, gets his sticky hands contaminated with insecticide and then licks his finger. Not a recommended diet.

Flea collars remain effective for about ten to twelve weeks. Regular renewal of the collar means that any flea that your cat collects during his wanderings is killed on arrival and has no opportunity to establish a new dynasty beneath your fitted carpets.

Dusting powder, or sprays or washes must be used to treat the cat's environment if fleas are a recurrent problem to your cat. Clean and wash the basket, and wash the blankets. No flea will survive a good washing-machine programme with all the magical washing powders now available. Newspaper is a very good substitute for blankets in the cat's bed. You can burn the newspaper daily and save the washing troubles.

A dust of powder on the carpets in the cat's sleeping areas is essential. There's no need to powder the whole house as a rule. If you watch your cat you'll find that he tends to have well-defined snoozing areas such as near a radiator or where the morning sun strikes the rug. Some dusting of these areas, and then a vacuuming, should spell death to any young fleas.

In extreme cases where there is gross infestation, fumigation is the only course available. This situation will never happen in your house if you treat the first flea seriously and deal with it long before a population has occurred. Very many insecticides are available. If you buy proprietary ones, make certain that they are suitable for cats, which are not always tolerant of powders intended for dogs or even cattle.

Lice

Lice sometimes infest cats, usually around the neck, head and ears. They are little grey/purple objects attached to the skin, not moving from place to place. They usually cause considerable irritation, but be-

cause lice spend all their life on their host, treatment—
and elimination—is easier than with flea infestation.
One very important factor is that, while lice are easy
to kill using a suitable insecticide, their eggs—nits—
are resistant. So a ten-day interval between skin dressings is important to allow the newly-hatched lice,
which were eggs at day one, to be killed before they
have had a chance to lay eggs at day ten. Some of
the washes made for use against the human head louse
are unsafe for cats. Make certain that anything you
use is meant for cats or, safer still, ask your vet to pre-
scribe or supply something suitable.

Ticks

Ticks occur occasionally. This is the so-called sheep
tick but its tastes are catholic and it is prepared to
attach itself to any available warm-blooded animal.
Ticks appear suddenly. The young tick is found in
rough grass or undergrowth. It attaches itself to a
passing animal and begins to feed on blood. As a result
the tick's body increases in size very rapidly and
within a few days may become the size of a small hari-
cot bean, and about the same shape. The mass of the
body is grey/white coloured and a dark-brown head
and legs can be seen close to the cat's skin.

Some cats take little notice of these parasites, others
appear to be violently irritated. In either case the ticks
are best not there, and if your cat is ever affected,
veterinary advice should be obtained. If, because you
live near tick-prone rough ground, ticks are a regular
occurrence on your cat, routine dressings of a long-
lasting insecticide can be obtained from your vet.

Ears

Reading this, you are unconscious of your ears, nose, eyes and all appendages unless something is wrong, such as a chilblain on your ear, or a corn on your big toe. Then you know you have an ear or a toe and react accordingly. So does your cat. The best indication of healthy ears in the cat is his ignoring them. Any scratching, any shaking of the head, holding the head to one side or rubbing it on the ground is a warning sign that all is not well. Any treatment of ear troubles must follow a diagnosis. It's very easy to name all ear discomfort 'canker'—and also very uninformative. Canker means, in this context, a bad ear. No more, no less. It's also a disease of horses' feet and apple trees, and it has no connection at all with cancer.

So-called 'canker' lotions might help a sore ear, if they happen to be the correct treatment for that particular ear disorder, but if the cause of the ear pain is not the particular one envisaged by the maker of the lotion, treatment will be ineffective.

Having said that, there is one important and common cause of ear problems. A mite called Otodectes is a very common invader of cats' ears. Many adult cats are amazingly tolerant of this mite. They scratch a bit more than normal, shake their heads sometimes, flatten the ears when stroked near the head, but otherwise show little reaction. If one of these cats becomes unwell, from any cause, the ear mites seem to get above themselves and this tolerance to their presence disappears leading to an acutely painful ear. Young kittens may collect mites from their mother at a very early age, and suffer much more than mum.

It's usually possible to see a dark-brown/mahogany wax in the ears of mite-affected cats. This wax is a reaction to the irritation of the mites—Nature's attempt to alleviate the situation. Mere removal of the wax will not help. The wax is a result of the ear trouble, not a cause of it.

By examining the ear using an auroscope—an illuminated device which allows your vet to see into the ear canal—the mites can be seen and there is no doubt about the cause, and hence the treatment, that is indicated.

This examination with an auroscope is essential in any ear condition. Apart from mites, bacterial infections, wart-like growths and foreign bodies can all cause similar symptoms of ear discomfort, pain or discharges and each one needs a different treatment.

One spectacular condition occurs on the ear flap as a result of ear irritation—a sudden (within twenty-four hours) swelling of the whole ear flap due to the bursting of a blood vessel between the layers of skin forming the ear. This is just the same happening as the boxer who gets a 'thick' ear. The cause is the same, external violence, except that the cat does it to himself by scratching or shaking. The proper name for this is a haematoma. Untreated, the thick ear turns into a cauliflower ear as the blood clot disappears and scar formation between the two layers of skin twists and deforms the normal ear shape—referring now to boxer or cat. But back to the cat. A haematoma is not usually painful, although the ear irritation that caused the shaking and scratching may be. No doubt the cat feels strange with this large ear flap which twenty-four hours earlier was much smaller.

Treatment of the cause, in the ear canal, as well as treatment of the effect, in the ear flap, is required. Operations to remove the blood clot will usually result in a much better-looking ear, slightly scarred but not a true cauliflower appearance. As well as the better cosmetic effect, surgical treatment of haema-

tomas prevents the badly-scarred ear from partly
blocking the ear canal and preventing ventilation.

These ear haematomas are not dangerous, but they
do cause a certain amount of panic to cat owners and
any operation is a slight upset to the cat. If you take
note of the first signs of ear discomfort, and get
advice and treatment at this early stage, most haematomas will not start because the prolonged scratching
and shaking that leads to breaking a blood vessel will
not occur.

Eyes

Like ears, good healthy eyes attract little attention. Any excess eye discharge, a closed or half-closed eye or pawing at eyes means trouble. Any eye abnormality needs fairly rapid and proper attention.

One eye condition attracts a lot of attention when it occurs but it is not really a sign of anything wrong with the eyes. This is protrusion of the third eyelids. On the *inside* corner of each eye is this third eyelid—also known as the nictitating membrane or the haw. Sometimes both third eyelids protrude to cover half the eyeball. They are white/pink in colour and protrude from the corner of the eye nearest the nose. Usually nothing is amiss in the eyes and the cat has not developed cataracts. The third eyelid is *on* the eyeball and outside it. Cataracts—which can occur in cats—are in the lens which is inside the eyeball.

Thus, no panic about loss of sight. The appearance of these third eyelids is an early warning sign that the cat is not quite 100 per cent fit. Sometimes no ill health can be recognized. Sometimes obvious illness appears after a day or so. If this ever happens to your cat and he seems fit in every other respect, wait, but watch him very closely. If he continues to thrive and there is no eye discharge, have patience. It may take three weeks or longer before the haws go back into their normal place.

If the cat appears unwell, of course, you must get advice from your vet, and all the above only applies if *both* eyes are affected. One of the functions of the third eyelid is to protect the eye, and if there is eye injury or damage, the third eyelid of that eye will come out to protect the injured surface of the eyeball. One haw showing is usually more serious than both.

Weepy eyes can occur in some cats, more often in

long-haired ones, because the tear duct is blocked. This is a tiny tube that runs from the inside corner of the eye socket into the back of the throat and is the drain pipe through which the normal tears flow away. If this drain is blocked, an overflow occurs and the tears run on to the face.

Diagnosis is reasonably simple. Your vet puts a tiny drop of fluorescent dye into the eye and within minutes this should appear on the roof of the mouth or in the nostril. Clearance of the blocked duct is sometimes possible, but this must be done under anaesthetic.

Teeth

The adult cat usually has thirty teeth. He starts life with twenty-six temporary (milk) teeth and changes all these and adds four to them by six months of age. This 'teething' rarely, if ever, presents difficulties and most cat owners don't notice the change.

Later in life, tooth troubles are quite common, not the decay from which we suffer and involving fillings, but infections of the gums and tooth sockets. The majority of dental problems in cats are caused by tartar accumulating on the teeth.

Tartar comes from salts in saliva and builds up on the teeth. Some cats are more prone to tartar production than others, but gross tartar accumulation can be prevented in the vast majority of cats by making them exercise their teeth.

Your cat will exercise his teeth by using them; make him clean them himself by driving them into, or rubbing them on to, an abrasive substance. Tearing meat off a bone, eating a *large* piece of meat, tearing it up first and chewing at dry cat food are examples of tooth exercise; so is catching, and eating, a bird, mouse or rabbit, and this explains the good teeth of most farm cats. A diet solely of tinned food or fish or cut-up meat is too easy to eat and the teeth are never cleaned by these very soft foods.

Tartar accumulates on the teeth and may form masses greater in size than the tooth itself. It rubs the gum and pushes the gum away from the tooth socket so that infection can develop and a loose tooth occurs because there is nothing to hold it in place.

The large canine (eye) teeth are sometimes broken in fights or car accidents. The cat looks a little odd with two up and one and a half down, but the broken tooth rarely if ever decays or causes pain.

Diagnosis of the actual problem is a job for your vet. Your responsibility as a concerned cat owner is to recognize the need for attention.

Become concerned if your cat shows that he knows he has a mouth or teeth. Pawing at the mouth, usually one side only, might indicate a loose tooth, excess tartar rubbing on the gum or something stuck in the mouth or on the teeth. Excess salivation is a common sign of mouth or tongue ulcers from infections or injury (cut tongues from tin cans are not at all uncommon) or loose teeth.

Many cats will salivate because of excitement—maybe panic, maybe ecstasy. The very friendly cat that jumps on your lap, is delighted to meet you and 'treads' with his fore feet will sometimes leave you with a very wet lap because his pleasure at meeting you is also shown by profuse salivation. Some highly nervous cats leave a pool of saliva on the consulting-room table when taken to the vet. No one has hurt them, no one has upset them, but these cats have met an unusual situation and panic produces saliva.

A problem cat is the one that salivates freely as soon as anyone opens his mouth to give him a pill. The thick saliva seems to get everywhere and dropping a pill into the back of the mouth is nearly impossible. It gets stuck in the thick saliva. This seems to happen to every vet when a client says, 'Will you show me how to give a tablet to the cat?' That cat is always the difficult, salivating one.

The excitement salivation is short-lasting and once you know your cat, you know what to expect. Salivation due to mouth disorders is persistent and usually accompanied by some signs of discomfort, especially when the cat tries to eat.

This chapter would not be complete without mentioning opening a cat's mouth, giving pills and medicines. Some owners find this difficult and we, vets, are sometimes guilty of dispensing tablets for a cat, happily writing the instructions 'Give one night and morning' without enquiring if the owner can give, or ever has given, a pill to his cat. The owner doesn't like to ask 'how?', and we don't show him. If in doubt, ask your vet to show how—and working as a vet, let me assure you that the moment we are asked to demonstrate, things are likely to go wrong; so if they do, be tolerant.

The first, near essential, part of giving medicine— or opening the mouth— is to have the cat in the right place. This is on a table or something similar with a smooth surface. The cat loses some confidence. You are working at a convenient height. Pill giving or mouth opening with the cat on your lap gives him an advantage in that your clothes—and flesh—provide a good grip for the claws. The table is slightly slippery so he can't grip. Hold the cat's head from behind, rather like gripping a cricket ball (left hand if you're right-handed); with the other hand firmly and gently open the mouth by pressure on the lower front teeth and gently push his cheeks, with finger and thumb of the left hand between the molar teeth at the side of the mouth. He won't bite his own cheek.

If you're giving a tablet, pull the head back so that his nose is facing the ceiling. Drop the tablet into the mouth and it will fall (gravity is a potent force) to the centre of the back of the tongue. Touch the tablet with your finger, or the blunt end of a pencil, and push it an extra quarter-inch. The cat will swallow. Tablet given.

Liquid medicines can be given without opening the mouth. Hold the cat in the same 'cricket ball' way and then make a pouch with the corner of the mouth and pour the medicine in this pouch. Let the cat do the swallowing. You merely place the liquid, a little

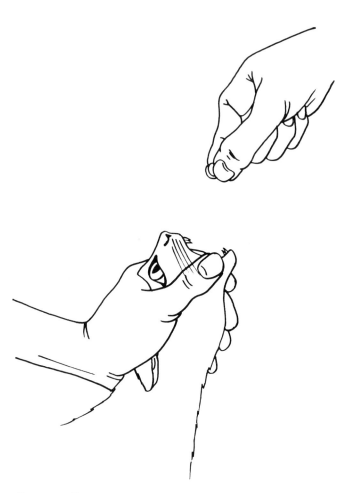

Giving pills

at a time, in the mouth. It's usually easier to give
liquids from a small bottle rather than a spoon. If
the cat struggles and hits the spoon, the liquid is
everywhere. If he hits the bottle very little spills out.

If you just want to look in his mouth as there may
be something stuck there, use the same method without any tablets.

Abscesses

Abscesses deserve a chapter of their own because they are so common. It may be that they represent the most numerous single cause of veterinary attention to cats. It's not that the cat as a species is particularly susceptible to infections, but cats fight, and bite, and the cat bite is a deep puncture wound which provides a marvellous breeding ground for pus-forming bacteria. Just look at your cat's teeth. The canine, or eye, teeth are long and pointed. In a fight these teeth puncture the skin, taking infection deep into the puncture wound. These infecting bacteria might come from the biter's teeth, or from the bitten cat's skin. In either event, bacteria are placed deep under the skin and into the muscle. The tiny bite wound heals over the top quite quickly. Maybe the bitten cat is a bit sore for a day from the mechanical injury of the bite, but that's all—so far. Within three or four days the bacteria inside the tiny wound have multiplied considerably. These bacteria have found themselves in their idea of the perfect environment—warm with lots of food—so they multiply. Hence an abscess.

How do you recognize it? The cat will be in pain and even try to bite you when you touch the affected area. If the abscess is developing in a leg, he'll be lame on that leg. He may spit and swear at himself as he moves. There will be some swelling, sometimes a lot. Apart from these signs around the abscess itself, the cat will be unwell, and sometimes very unwell, because there may be some degree of generalized blood poisoning.

Treatment is essential. Antibiotic injections or tablets will usually deal with an abscess if used at an early stage, but if large amounts of pus have been formed, some type of operation to open the abscess and drain out the pus is essential. An untreated one, or one that is treated too late, will burst. Once this happens, the pain is relieved to a great extent and the cat feels much better, and you may feel that a trip to the vet has been avoided. Unfortunately, this recovery is often temporary. The abscess has burst through a small hole, a lot of pus has got away but not all. The small hole heals leaving some infection still imprisoned, and within days another painful abscess has developed.

That is, briefly, abscesses. But why do cats fight and bite each other so often? There are two main reasons— Sex and Territory—which are probably the same two reasons for most of the wars we humans have fought in the past centuries. The roaming tom cat fights— most viciously—for his ladies, and is not averse to a punch-up with any neutered cat, male or female, whose path he crosses. The un-neutered tom is well equipped for fighting; he's leaner and harder than his neutered brother and kitted with thick leathery skin around the neck and face which will bend hypodermic needles and protects this area from opponents' teeth. Neutered cats fight to protect their territory. Your cat will 'own' a certain area, which will not necessarily correspond with that area marked in red on the deeds of your house. He may share this area with one or two of the cats belonging to you or your neighbours, but he will defend it against feline interlopers, be they new arrival, neutered, owned cats or free-living, wandering tom cats.

What can you do to protect your cat? There's no one action that will prevent fights and abscesses. If you *know* your cat has been bitten within the past twenty-four hours, your vet may well be able to give an antibiotic injection which will prevent an abscess developing because of that particular bite, but there are no permanent preventive injections available.

Providing a place of retreat can help. This may be a cat-door so that your cat can get back to his house, or if this is not possible a cat-door into a garden shed or garage will help. It is very unlikely that the attacking cat will follow him indoors. Many cat owners have problems of peripatetic cats coming indoors through the cat-flap and leaving tom cat smells behind. In the majority of cases the visiting cat is looking for, and finding, food. If you decide to fit a cat-door, a lot of problems are avoided if you take care that food is not available for visitors.

If, in spite of this, you are troubled by strange cats using your cat's entrance, a solution is to keep the door closed for a fortnight. This is inconvenient and unfortunate for your cat, who cannot understand being kept in, but usually successful in persuading the unwelcome visitor to transfer his affections elsewhere. Some sophisticated cat-flaps are operated by an electronic device on your cat's collar so the door remains firmly shut to other cats.

Skin troubles

Cats may develop bald patches, itchy patches or ulcerated patches on their skin. Self-inflicted scratching or licking will remove hair and create quite extensive inflamed areas of skin. The causes of such skin troubles are legion and treatment must always be based on a diagnosis of the individual cat's problem— which means the cat seeing a veterinary surgeon and, more important, the vet seeing the cat. If 'do-it-yourself' treatments ever work on skin disorders, it is usually by sheer chance.

One skin infection, happily not common, is transmissible to humans. Ringworm occurs in cats and can be passed to people. Often there are few signs to be seen on the cat and suspicions are only aroused when ringworm is diagnosed on someone in the family. Should this unlikely event happen, make sure that your doctor and veterinary surgeon talk to each other; firstly to make sure that the skin disease in the human is positively confirmed as ringworm—not merely suspected amongst other non-transmissible infections. Secondly, if the precise type of ringworm is established, your vet will know what type to look for in the cat, and what particular techniques to use in his search.

Treatment of ringworm is possible, but if human infection is involved it is often wise to have the cat hospitalized until treatment is finished so that recurrent infections cannot occur.

Combing

If you have any hair left in these troubled times, you comb it frequently. As your cat neither votes, pays taxes nor worries about the future, he will have plenty of hair—and it needs combing. Long-haired cats must be combed regularly. Not to do so is as much neglect as not feeding them. Short-haired cats require less combing and many go from one year's end to the next, never having seen a comb. But there are times, either when the coat is being shed, or when the cat grows old and careless of his toilet, that combing is essential for the ordinary short-hair.

Notice COMBING. Your cat might enjoy being brushed; brushing might make a well-combed cat look even smarter; but combing is the type of grooming that is essential for cats. There are two main reasons for combing, to remove tangles and knots from the coat and to remove dead hair. No matter how much you comb you will only take out dead hair. If your cat appears to be becoming a bit thin on top after a good combing, don't feel that you have caused this baldness. All that you have done is to make it evident. If anything is wrong you have discovered it sooner and if there is a great mass of dead hair it's possible that once the cat's skin finds out that it's got colder (because the dead coat isn't keeping it warm) there will be more encouragement to grow a nice new *living* coat.

Combing also allows you to check for fleas. By looking at the hair-filled comb you can detect either fleas—if there are a lot present—or tiny black specks which are flea faeces.

How to comb—in three words—with some vigour. Make certain that you are combing through the coat,

not merely passing over the surface. Your cat may
not enjoy it, he might protest, he might struggle, he
might scratch. If you were combing the tangled hair
of a difficult child, you would not stop combing when
the child 'Ouched', 'Ow'd' or wriggled. You would
explain that sitting quietly would help, that co-opera-
tion would mean that the whole dreadful business
would finish quicker, or you would slap the child—
your reaction depending on your temperament and
temper. A similar firmness of approach to the unco-
operative cat works just as well. Slapping isn't any
use, but a firm grip of the scruff of the neck and a
bit of a shake have the same effect on a self-
opinionated cat as a slap has on a self-opinionated
child. NEVER stop combing because the cat
struggles. You are teaching him that struggling pays
off. Stop combing only when you have finished—or
if exhaustion sets in—when there is a period of good
behaviour. Teach him that good behaviour (or
patient resignation, however the cat sees it) gets its
due reward.

Furballs.   Talk of combing leads to talk of furballs.
This is a sudden journey from the outside of the cat,
where the fur is, to the inside, the stomach and intestines, where the fur shouldn't be, but that's just
what happens in furballs.

All cats wash themselves—an admirable habit—but
don't always know when to stop and, as a result, can
swallow considerable quantities of dead hair. This
hair gets into the stomach and the normal churning
movements of the stomach turn it into masses rather
like hair sausages. Such bulky, foreign material is not
to the liking of the average stomach and in many
cases the inevitable happens: the cat vomits and the
furball is expelled. No harm done—unless the hairy
mess lands at your feet during a polite tea party—

but even then no harm is done to the cat. The stomach has been emptied of this unsuitable, indigestible material and all is back to normal.

Furballs cause trouble when they are not vomited, when the mass of hair passes along the digestive tract from the stomach into the narrower tube of the intestines to cause a partial or complete blockage. In the extreme case of total blockage, surgical removal of the furball may be required. Much more often the effect is to cause chronic constipation—everything moves through the intestines at a very slow pace. One can imagine the cat feeling 'overfull'. Result—lethargy, poor appetite and vomiting after food, nature's reaction being 'There's enough in the digestive tract already', so out comes the food.

Good, regular combing prevents the vast majority of furballs. If there is mild furball trouble, a dose of liquid paraffin (dose being about a teaspoonful) will often oil the intestinal tubes so that a slow-moving furball is eased out and troubles are over. Don't blame furballs for all non-eating and coughing illnesses. In fact be very certain that a furball is the cause of any trouble before deciding on 'do-it-yourself' treatment, and certainly never give any violent purgative such as castor oil to a cat that you think has a furball. Liquid paraffin cannot harm, it merely oils, and no matter how much you give the only problem that is created is for you when the oil leaks from the blunt end of the cat and leaves an oily patch on the carpet every time he sits down.

Collars

We've talked about flea collars, what about identification collars? Every dog should have one, but very few cats wear one. If any animal goes astray the finder can always tell the owner, if he knows who that owner is. The lost animal cannot help. There is the story of the card in the shop window.

Found, tabby kitten, white paws. Answers to the name of 'Go away'.

If your cat wears a flea collar, it's well worth writing your name and phone number on any part of the collar that will receive it; alternatively a name disc could be attached.

If you don't use or don't need a flea collar on your cat, should he wear a collar with your name? It is said that there is a danger of getting caught in trees. Many collars have pieces of elastic in them to stop this danger. This is a subject on which it's difficult to advise; there are risks versus benefits. You will have to make your own decision.

Bells are often used on collars so that birds will be given advance warning and the cat foiled. It's a sign of a very nice nature in the cat owner to add a bell to the collar and certainly mice will be forewarned, but most birds rely on sight rather than sound for their alarm system. It is only the sunlight on a shiny bell that is going to give them that few seconds start.

Accidents

Even the most domesticated cat is a free agent, under his own control for much of the time, and as he lives in a man-made environment, unnatural hazards are always present. The worst of these are motor cars, and very serious injuries, or death, may occur when a cat collides with a motor car.

Before talking about the types of 'run-overs' that happen, there is a basic philosophy concerning cats and cars that is worth considering. Cats enjoy freedom, freedom to wander, freedom to do their own thing. All freedoms involve dangers and the one must balance the other. It seems reasonable to accept that the cat that is allowed freedom is at risk, but restraint, which the cat might construe as imprisonment, makes life so boring and unacceptable to the average cat that it is reasonable to allow him the run-over risk. One can sometimes be critical of a dog owner if his dog is run over. It should not have been on the highway off a lead, but the cat keeper's responsibility in this respect is quite different.

There are other risks to the independent cat. Dog-caused injuries occur, although most active cats are quite capable of avoiding—or defeating—the 'Auld enemy'. Foxes are blamed for killing cats. How much good evidence there is for this belief is open to doubt. Certainly a fox might take an already dead cat, and eat it, possibly a very hungry fox might kill a tiny kitten or a very ill or old and defenceless cat. The average town fox has good pickings from dustbins and does not need, or feel inclined, to tackle anything as sharp as a cat. Many stories of cat and fox are third, fourth or fifth hand. Others are first hand but consist of finding cat remains outside a fox's earth, with no evidence that the fox did anything but find a dead, probably run-over, cat. There are chicken and lamb bones in my dustbin; this does not indicate who killed the bird or the lamb. If your cat is fit and over six months old, foxes are more likely to cause you an ulcer (from worry) than injure the cat. Town foxes respect the fighting abilities of cats.

Motor-car injuries vary enormously in their severity. Broken legs can usually be treated and modern surgery gives perfect or near perfect recovery in the majority of cases. These modern methods involve the use of metal plates or rods (known as pins) which are attached to the bone in the case of plates, or through the broken bones when pins are used.

Fractures of the pelvis are common. An X-ray is often needed to confirm this diagnosis, but in very many cases a good recovery results without surgical treatment. Cats are agile and patient. The cat suffering from a fractured pelvis will remain immobile for three weeks or so while the fractures heal.

The tail may be paralysed, lying completely limp as a consequence of pelvic fracture, and a similar tail paralysis can occur as the only result of an accident. Recovery may take as long as three weeks, but some cases never recover. If the tail remains paralysed it has to be amputated. No cat can be left indefinitely with a totally paralysed tail. He will drag it along the ground and damage it. Faeces become stuck to the hair of the tail. He may set it on fire or get it caught in a door without having the 'alarm' sensation of pain to provide natural protection.

Clean amputation, before the tail is badly infected, is infinitely preferable to an emergency operation on a grossly diseased tail.

Head, face and jaw injuries are common in cat and motor car collisions, and amazingly rare in dog/car incidents. The degree of injury in the cat varies from fatal head damage to eye injuries and broken upper or lower jaws.

One probable explanation of this cat/dog difference is their reaction when in danger. A cat may tend to 'freeze' and squat. The car wheels pass either side of the cat, but a projecting piece of chassis, exhaust pipe or similar, catches the motionless cat a glancing blow on the head. A dog faced with a similar situation carries on running and either escapes altogether or is hit by the body, wheel or bumper. This explanation is speculative; no one really sees such accidents. If there are 'eye-witnesses' they only see what has happened, one second later, and every vet has seen the dog or cat alleged to have been run over by a motor car 'and the wheel passed over his head'. Examination of the unlucky animal might show that the only injury is on the tip of the tail.

Cuts—from what we know not—are often seen. The owner always wishes to know 'How did it happen?', which, if you reflect, is of academic interest only. One suggests glass, tins, and again motor cars, but any answer is only speculation.

Traps and snares catch cats. Gin traps are illegal, but are still seen; they cause serious crushing wounds to the feet. Snares, as used, are often set illegally and the wire can cut into the neck, the chest or leg. One other seemingly harmless material can cut into legs, tails and necks—rubber, in the form of elastic bands. One never knows who puts them onto the cat; it is certainly not a cat-inflicted accident. Hopefully it is very young children who know no better. However it gets there, an elastic band around a leg or the neck will cut deeply into and sometimes through the skin, leading to a lot of pain, a lot of treatment after the elastic is removed, and even loss of a leg if neglected.

Scalds by boiling water or hot fat happen in the

kitchen. These are usually the fault of a greedy cat getting under the cook's feet, but a bad scald is an over-severe punishment for greed. Cat hair gives the skin a limited degree of protection, but also keeps the hot water or fat in contact with the skin for a minute or so after the incident. Immediate emergency treatment of lots of cold water will cool down the skin and hair as quickly as possible. The scalded cat will never co-operate in this first aid but if you can catch the very frightened cat and douse him with cold water on the affected area, it will help. Anything other than a trivial scald needs veterinary attention at an early stage.

Other liquids are spilt on cats, or cats fall into them. Some substances such as creosote, turpentine and paraffin will kill cats, partly by absorption through the skin and partly by the oil being swallowed when the cat cleans himself.

Emergency treatment is important here. Bathing is vital. Lots and lots of water is needed, with washing-up liquid, hair shampoo or toilet soap. Wash the cat until all traces of the creosote, oil or what-have-you are removed. 'Swarfega', often used by car enthusiasts, is safe for cats covered in oil.

Bathing a cat is quite possible and relatively easy if you set about it the right way. Lift the cat on to a smooth surface; the draining board is excellent. Put a temporary collar round the cat's neck; a piece of tape or bandage tied with a *non* slip knot works well. You'll find this collar useful when you try to hold a wet, soapy, slippery cat.

Half-fill the sink with pleasantly warm water (about 80°F or 27°C, if you must take the temperature). While the cat is still on the draining board wet and soap him all over, using an unbreakable container such as a plastic cup or jug. Most cats are fairly miserable about the whole proceeding, but accept it. On

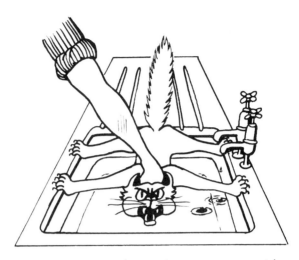

Any attempt to put a dry cat in water meets with much more resistance

the other hand, any attempt to put a dry cat into water meets with much more resistance. When the cat is wet and soapy from stem to stern, put him in the water to rinse. An already wet cat does not resent partial immersion nearly as much as a dry one.

When you're holding the cat, during bathing or at any other time, a slight downward pressure on the head, so that he cannot 'climb', keeps him restrained. Any frightened struggling cat always tries to raise his head and go upwards. If you stop him starting the movement, he can't try.

Back to bathing. Once the cat is rinsed and free from soap—and whatever else you are trying to remove—dry him with towels or a hair dryer. If you are using a dryer, remember to keep it moving so there is no danger of over-heating wet fur and producing a burn or scald.

Keep the cat indoors for a few hours if there's a cold east wind, but don't worry about pneumonia as a result of bathing; it won't happen. Neither will he

Any frightened cat always tends to ... go upwards

stop cleaning himself. In fact, the very dirty cat, with
his coat covered in some objectionable substance,
may not wash himself while he's very dirty. It tastes
horrible and the cat becomes discouraged. Once you
have helped to clean him up, he takes new heart.

Most cats live their whole life and never need a
bath. It is only in special situations that a wash is
indicated. Friday night is not every cat's bath night.

Poisons

Cats are easily poisoned in so far as some substances which are relatively safe to dogs, horses and humans are particularly toxic to cats. Benzoic acid, sometimes used as a food preservative, and creosote are two examples. Some of the common skin dressings used for dogs may cause illness if used on cats.

Poisons

As well as being extra sensitive, cats are susceptible to poisons absorbed from the skin. This can either be by direct absorption through the skin or by swallowing something that has contaminated the fur.

There is another, brighter, side to the poisoning coin. Cats are choosy feeders. In contrast to this fastidious approach puppies like to chew anything—

because they like to chew. Cows are such inquisitive animals that they eat things as part of their investigation. So Granny's pills, in their child-proof container, poison puppies, and plastic sacks appear in cows' stomachs.

Cats eat poisons, the commonest being rat and mouse poisons. There are several useful rules here. If you are using these place them very carefully out of any cat's way. For outdoor use, a large stone paving slab raised some 2 inches above the ground by four solid stones provides a safe area. A small quantity of mouse bait under the slab is out of the reach of any cat. This is also a safe way to use slug pellets. A long thin drainpipe with the poison halfway along is another cat-safe arrangement.

Always read the instructions carefully before use; then keep the packet which contained the rodent poison so that if any accident should occur, you can help by telling your vet what poison was used. Better still, take the packet to the vet.

If anyone else is using poison, be he Council Rodent Operative or Pest Officer or a neighbour, find out, and write down, what poison is being used and insist that it is placed safely. If rat control is taking place next door, and your cat 'owns' this land, you must keep him in. A miserable, disgruntled, housebound cat is preferable to a dead one.

The commonest mouse poison involved is, fortunately, rarely fatal to cats. It is called alphachloralose but is sold under various proprietary names; it is an anaesthetic. Because the mouse is such a small animal, his surface area is very large compared to his bulk and so an anaesthetized mouse loses heat very quickly and dies from cold while unconscious. This is very effective and humane. It doesn't work so well (anti-mice) in hot weather or in centrally heated buildings where the mouse can curl up beside a hot water pipe when

A disgruntled housebound cat is preferable to a dead one

he feels sleepy and wake up twenty-four hours later with nothing worse than a bad hangover.

If a cat eats alphachloralose he becomes anaesthetized to a greater or lesser degree depending on his size and the amount eaten. He may either go into the excitement stage (such as you might experience when having 'gas' at a dentist's) or, if enough has been eaten, into deep unconsciousness. Fortunately, the larger size of a cat compared with a mouse means slower heat loss, the great majority of cats suffering in this way recover within forty-eight hours with not much more treatment than warmth. No doubt the cat's fond owner suffers more, so caution with mouse poisons, even those as relatively safe as alpha-chloralose, is well advised.

One final note about alphachloralose—cats like it
and, having been resurrected after one dose, are quite
likely to go back the next day to the poison source
for another feed.

Any poisoning needs veterinary treatment. The
only first-aid measures are washing if a poisonous
substance is on the coat, or an emetic, if a poison
has just been swallowed. For any emetic to be of real
use it must be given within ten to fifteen minutes of
eating the poison. The most effective home-remedy
emetic is washing soda. A piece the size of a broad
bean, given as if it were a tablet, will cause vomiting
within a few minutes and, if given in time, can save
a cat's life.

Claws

There are four main claws on each foot and a dew-claw (the equivalent of our thumb) on the front legs. At rest and when walking about the claws are retracted and only extended during a fight, when climbing or gripping something, or when 'clawing' at that new uncut moquette suite.

There is no need to cut the claws of 'free living' cats. A cat will keep them worn to size during his excursions around your, and neighbours', gardens and his journeys up and down trees. A very old cat, snoozing in the sun and taking little exercise, may develop very long nails and catch them in carpets or become hung up on furniture; these nails do need

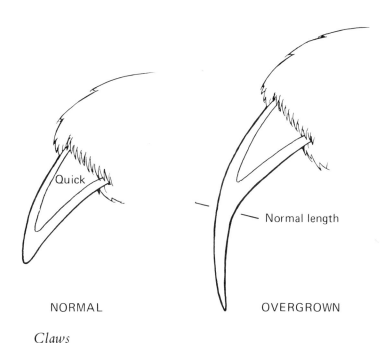

Quick

NORMAL

Normal length

OVERGROWN

Claws

cutting. Any cat with extra nails might well require
regular pedicures throughout his life.

How do you decide if nails need attention? Look at
them; put the cat on a table and examine each foot.

Back feet usually have shorter nails than front feet.
It is quite possible to cut the nails yourself; the quick
is easily visible, as a pink core. Use proper nail
clippers. If in doubt ask your vet to show you.

Any talk about nails would be incomplete without
an attempt to answer that plaintive cry: 'How do I
stop my cat from sharpening his claws on the
furniture?' Unfortunately the practical reply must
be: 'You probably won't stop him; what a pity you
let him start.'

It is possible to persuade a young kitten that a
particular piece of wood or surplus carpet nailed on

Sharpening his claws on the furniture

to the leg of the kitchen table is his scratching post, and everywhere else is forbidden ground. Owners who achieve this near miracle are exceptional cat owners and the cats who learn this must be exceptionally gifted cats.

Once scratching has started, the only action you can take is to cover the furniture, if possible, for some months so that the cat will look for something else. Provide something like a sawn log or piece of carpet. Tell him, vocally, and by picking him up and removing him, that it's wrong to scratch the furniture. It is possible to practise aversion therapy if you are a good shot with a water pistol. Use it to give him a jet of cold clean water every time he scratches the upholstery. (Providing the colours are waterproof). He will begin to associate the furniture with an unpleasant experience, and avoid scratching it, but he won't start to hate you. But be warned, cats don't try to learn to please their owners—dogs do, and want to do the right thing; cats do their own thing.

You must accept a bit of extra wear and tear on furniture and the odd nibble of the house plants. If you can't, keep tropical fish instead of a cat.

Breeding

We are not talking about pedigree cat breeding so the first step in this process, mating, does not concern us. If you have an un-neutered queen as a pet she is almost certain to mate at the first opportunity, and conceive. Like every liberated female she will not consult anyone, least of all you, about her choice of mate.

Step one takes place without your prior knowledge. However, you should have registered that the cat is 'calling'. The unmistakable signs have been described earlier in the section 'Neutering'. Make a note of the date. Gestation is about 63 days, thus a very simple calculation will tell you when kittens can be expected. *About* 63 days—which means that some cats kitten sooner and some later—so if your cat carries her kittens past the 63rd day she is not wrong.

Worry—and do something—if your cat seems unwell, seems unable to deliver a kitten, if she's straining, if she's off food or if she has a discharge. But not if she is just a bad mathematician.

Most cats have their kittens unaided without any human interference. Maybe she is less than a year old, maybe she has no experience, certainly she has not read all about it. *But* she is quite capable of coping very well if you let her, and if you are there as a 'back up' in the very rare circumstance of complications during birth.

Provide a kittening box. This need be nothing more complicated or expensive than a cardboard box about 2 feet square. Make it as private as possible so that the mother-to-be feels secure.

Newspaper is one of the best bedding materials. Blankets and towels are difficult to wash and very young kittens can become entangled in woollen or cotton materials and the mother cat might squash them.

Normal kittening takes place quietly. The queen will retire to her box and probably refuse food. She will cope with afterbirths and umbilical cords. Signs of difficulties are prolonged straining, no kittens appearing, or a kitten being partly expelled and, in spite of the mother's efforts, birth proceeds no further.

If you think that things are not proceeding normally phone your vet and be prepared to take the cat to his surgery. Phone first—it may be that you are being a little impatient, and he may advise a wait of an hour or so. Such advice does not mean that your vet is disinterested, it stems from the fact that every vet would rather see a normal kittening take place, without interference, than do an unnecessary operation.

If there is difficulty the vet's surgery is the proper place to rectify it. Caesarian operations are usually very successful, but these are best done in proper conditions rather than on your kitchen table. If only a minor degree of help is needed to deliver a kitten there is help available at the surgery. Any kittening results in a certain amount of blood and a dark green/black colour is usual for the edges of the afterbirths. This colour can appear alarming if you see it for the first time as a stain on white newspaper. It is perfectly normal.

If you are a totally inexperienced feline midwife a visit (with the cat) to your vet ten days or so before kittening can be time well spent. Pregnancy can be confirmed—if there is any doubt—the cat will be examined and, very rarely, some difficulty anticipated. Most importantly you can be helped by talking about normal kittening and discovering also what 'out of social hours' arrangements are should your cat decide to kitten in the wee small hours—and need attention.

A fringe benefit can sometimes be that your vet knows of homes for the kittens. Don't complain if he doesn't, most vets are inundated with requests to find homes for kittens. You should look ahead also. Kittens are ready to leave mother at seven to eight weeks of age. Time passes quickly so look for homes for them as soon as they are born. Your vet can help you by telling you the local kitten supply and demand situation. If there are a lot more kittens than homes, consider keeping only two and having the others destroyed soon after birth. It should not need a mention, but do have them put to sleep in a humane fashion, *not* drowned.

If a litter of kittens exhausts you, if you have run out of homes for the kittens, you may decide to have your cat spayed after one litter. A she cat usually starts calling again about ten days after the kittens have left home and even if you keep a kitten she will come on heat about ten to twelve weeks after the kittens were born. If you want to avoid the next litter make arrangements for spaying in good time— next week might be too late.

How to take your cat to the vet

Before 'How', let's consider 'When'.

Whenever you are concerned, worried or unhappy about your cat's well-being is the correct time to consult your veterinary surgeon. 'Consult' may mean in the first instance simply phoning him to say, 'My cat has . . .; does it matter? Is it serious?' There is no need to preface this enquiry with 'I'm sorry to bother you'. Vets exist to be consulted. They would starve otherwise, so if you feel that your worry is too trivial to justify veterinary time, think again.

It is a perfectly good and proper use of veterinary time to be told 'There's nothing wrong, it's quite normal; don't worry.' You as a conscientious cat owner have enquired—your duty. The vet has examined and answered—his duty.

So 'when' is when you are worried and of course for routine vaccinations and neutering.

How do you get your cat to the surgery? In a cat box or cat basket might seem a 'flip' answer but it is worth saying. A number of cat owners drive to the surgery with the cat loose in the car, and then walk up the path and sit in the waiting room with the cat draped across their knees or wrapped around their neck. This is not the best way. Motor insurance companies do not look kindly upon claims based on 'the cat jumped on my lap'. Veterinary surgeons do not begrudge the Elastoplast needed when the frightened cat takes a tighter claw hold on the owner's neck, but the owner doesn't enjoy the experience. Every so often the cat gets out of the car before the owner— and there's another lost cat.

Boxes and baskets come in all sizes and at all prices. Simplest and cheapest are the *cardboard cat carriers*, 'Pet Packs', 'Pussy Packs'. These are often obtainable from your vet. They cost about £2, cheap enough to throw away if the container gets wet or dirty. Here's one tip for using these cardboard cat boxes: do NOT enlarge the air holes. There is plenty of air for every cat; if you make the holes larger you merely make a more convenient place for your cat to get a good claw hold to tear the cardboard to shreds.

Wicker baskets are the traditional type of cat basket. They are warm but difficult to clean. Beware of some of the oval or circular ones; the lid does not fasten well and a determined cat can force his way out. Be selfish if you own one. Don't lend it to all and sundry. First, it's never home when you need to use it and, secondly, they are difficult to clean, so it's not very good hygiene.

Metal baskets are usually plastic-covered wire. They are strong and easily cleaned. Many cats appear to accept these baskets because they allow the cat to see out. They are costly, about £15–£20, but long-lasting.

Plastic cat carriers of various types are also available. Some are very good with perspex sides so that you can see the cat and the cat can see everything. There are no draughts and it is nice and cosy for the cat. Usually they are easy to clean but they are sometimes quite expensive, at least £30.

Like so many things in life, you pays your money and you takes your choice.

Whatever choice you make, do not half-fill the basket with cushions, blankets or old cardigans before putting the cat in. Newspaper is the very best bedding. It's clean, cheap and warm. Just try putting today's paper on the floor. Within a very few minutes your cat will sit on the paper. This might be rather inconvenient if someone wants to read it, but it shows cats like newspaper.

Some cats must get a stiff neck after a sojourn in a basket so full of blanket or cushion that insufficient room is left for the cat. If there is a liquid or semi-solid accident, newspaper is absorbent and easier to get rid of than a well-perfumed cushion or cardigan.

These comments apply to all travelling—to kennels, moving house or going on holiday. Some cats are less than totally happy in a basket and say so noisily—which leads to tranquillizers, without which modern civilized man could not survive. While one can only be sad about the fact that many of the superior beings —the human race—think they have to live in a tranquillized state, the same considerations need not apply to your cat. Extreme cases need extreme measures, but every cat travelling for half an hour does not need to be tranquillized to undertake this journey.

... every cat travelling for half an hour does not need to be tranquillized ...

Apart from any ethical arguments, one practical point emerges. You cannot switch off a tranquillizer, so the cat that is given a sedative for travelling is only 99 per cent for the next twenty-four hours. He might lose a fight that he would have won—or run away from; he might come into collision with a motor car he would otherwise have avoided. It's not unreasonable to say to your cat, 'There's a less than pleasant two hours ahead of you, but it will end; put up with it.'

Here ends the sermon! To return to the subject of your vet and 'How?' You want to get good value from your vet, and this means asking questions. Vets are skilful people and most vets in general practice become skilled in knowing what worries owners. But few vets become mind readers. If you have a worry or a problem, ASK. In almost every case you'll get a helpful, reassuring answer. If the answer is what you feared, the sooner you know, the better, but no vet can answer a question that isn't asked.

Old age

If you have had a cat for years, the time comes when he has grown old, very old. He's wearing out and reaching true senile decay. Is it reasonable to keep him? ASK. Your vet will help. You must decide.

Old-age problems occur only in man and the protected animals. Farm animals become uneconomic as they age and so are slaughtered for economic reasons. Wild animals become incapable of surviving and starve or are killed by predators or their own kind when they grow old. Nature started 'putting to sleep' when time began, but in a rather crude way.

Old age does not happen suddenly, it's not a disease but certain parts of the body wear more quickly than others. The living body is a balanced entity, each part dependent on the others. If the heart is not pumping as well as it should, the lungs and the liver receive less blood than they should, and suffer accordingly. If the kidneys do not do their job of removing waste from the blood stream the brain, digestion and the mouth may be affected.

One of the commonest signs of senility is loss of weight, often with an increased thirst for water. Sometimes this is a thirst for stale or dirty water. The cat will ignore milk, ignore a bowl of clean fresh water and go in search of a puddle of rain water or drink from a fish pond, the drains or the water in a bowl of flowers.

Such a thirst may be Nature's attempt to help failing kidneys (sometimes, not always, for there are very many other causes of excessive drinking) by the flushing action of a lot of water allowing rather more waste to be eliminated from an inefficient kidney.

Let's repeat, old age does not happen suddenly. So if your elderly cat starts to lose weight and drink rather more, it does not mean his end is near. Treatment can often make the wearing parts (be they kidneys, heart, liver or what has he) work a bit better so that a pain-free, pleasurable life can continue for some time.

Geriatric care includes nursing. The old cat will appreciate three or four small meals per day, not more food but the same daily total spread out. Not only will this help his digestion but it will give more 'point' to the day. If he has a favourite sleeping chair he will appreciate some help if jumping up has become difficult. A strategically placed footstool might be a tactful way of convincing him that he's as fit as he ever was.

The failing cat cannot fight, or run, as he could in his salad days. Make certain he can get home into safety quickly if the younger neighbourhood cats decide to extend their territory and are prepared to fight for it.

Only start treatment and nursing if you are certain that it's for the cat's benefit.

If you have any animal, although we are talking about cats, that has ceased to enjoy life, is only surviving because you are providing, and is living for your pleasure and not its own, please give it a clean end and don't let it live for your sake only.

Fees

Vets' fees must be mentioned because some animals still remain untreated because owners are frightened of the cost. Fees vary from practice to practice and place to place. Any national standard fee would be illegal. As a guide £5–£10 covers the average surgery consultation plus average cost of drugs. House visits are more expensive, less than the man who comes to mend your washing machine or television set and the service is much quicker, but a visit will cost about £15–£25 in normal working hours and more if your cat needs attention in the small hours.

Insurance to cover veterinary costs is available; the premium is about £30 per year, less than that for the washing machine. It's a worthwhile safety net. Ask your vet about it – he'll probably have proposal forms from one or two of the companies that offer this service. They all vary a little, so read them carefully and see which policy fits your needs.

Bad habits

Spraying urine in the most inconvenient places is a territory marking device used by cats of both sexes, and by those neutered ones of neither. This bad habit is most common in the un-neutered male, and the problem is compounded by the pungent smell of tom cat urine.

It has been said that nearly 25 per cent of cats 'spray' at some time in their life, although this may only be as one single incident.

Treatment with various hormones often stops this trouble. Removing or covering the 'sprayed' object might prevent a habit developing, but a few cats remain constant sprayers, at inconstant intervals and treatment is not wholly effective.

Digging. If you or your neighbours are keen gardeners the beautiful seed beds that you prepare in the spring are an invitation to any cat. The nice, warm, dry soil is made for digging holes, and thus the seeds that were sown in straight lines eventually appear as clusters, if at all. Try offering an even more attractive convenience such as a large box of peat and earth, drier and softer. Small-mesh wire over the seed bed helps to divert the cat, but then the young plants become entangled in it. It's said that dry holly leaves spread over the seed bed work, but who has enough dry holly leaves?

Bird catching is a natural activity for every cat. He's not wicked, cruel, evil, just a normal, active cat. It's strange that the cat owner who verbally chastises his cat after a successful bird hunt, congratulates him if the victim is a mouse or, better still, a rat.

Nevertheless most people prefer their cat not to

catch birds. Achieving this is difficult. The commonly used bell on a collar is not likely to be very effective. Birds rely on sight as their early warning system—watch the next pigeon, eyes placed well to the side of the head, and a constant rotation of the neck means that he's watching all around. The tinkle of a tiny bell is unlikely to attract any bird's attention.

Bird tables need some sort of anti-cat verandah around the pole to foil the climbing cat, and if you provide bird nesting boxes make sure that they are well secured so that the strongest and heaviest cat cannot dislodge them.

Fighting

Other people's cats fight, yours defends himself.

The law

Finally, the LAW, which intrudes everywhere. This is not a legal treatise and anything that follows is 'without prejudice', but little follows.

The law hardly recognizes the cat. You must not import one without quarantine of six months (Rabies Act 1974). Boarding kennels for cats must be licensed by the District Council (Animal Boarding Establishments Act 1963). The cat is protected as are all other animals by the Protection of Animals Act 1911, which basically prohibits anything that causes unnecessary suffering.

Otherwise the cat occupies a unique position in that its owner is not responsible for the consequences of its trespass—lucky cat.

Its owner is not responsible for the consequence of its trespass

Index

Index by Northgate House

Also published by Sheldon Press

A PET DOG OF YOUR OWN

James Allcock

Foreword by Michael Stockman,
President of the British Veterinary Association (1979)

This is a book for every dog owner, especially the inexperienced. The author, a vet with thirty years' experience, starts at square one: should you own a dog at all?

From there he answers questions about the sex you should choose and where to buy your puppy. He removes the mystery from pedigrees, inoculations, feeding, spaying. He tells you when to worry and when not; how to avoid common troubles; how to deal with worms and fleas; and about breeding. A book to help anyone who cares about his dog to keep that dog better, healthier and happier.

A BVA Pet Care Book

Illustrated

ISBN 0 85969 164 0